JAMES BUCHANAN

A Life from Beginning to End

Copyright © 2021 by Hourly History.

All rights reserved.

Table of Contents

Introduction

The future 15th president of the United States, James Buchanan Jr., came into this world on April 23, 1791. He was the son of a Pennsylvania farmer, also named James Buchanan, and his wife Elizabeth. Mr. and Mrs. Buchanan lived in the quaint confines of Cove Gap, Pennsylvania, where they would raise a family of eleven children, of which James was the eldest son.

As well as farming, the Buchanans ran a successful family store. Through persistent hard work and dedication, they would go on to become one of the most prosperous families in Cove Gap. Besides tending to the family farm and store, young James went to school at the Old Stone Academy, where he received a basic education of reading, writing, and arithmetic.

It is said that he was an excellent student, and it was with his good grades, as well as his family's financial support, that the young James was eventually sent off to Dickinson College, located in the Pennsylvanian town of Carlisle. Here James Buchanan's status as a good student would be tarnished when he received an expulsion for bad behavior. It seems that James got caught up with the wrong crowd at Carlisle, and among the bad acts attributed to Buchanan and his school friends were drinking at the local bars, throwing food in the school's cafeteria, and various acts of vandalism around town.

Why did James Buchanan, a previously model student, resort to all this rabble-rousing? Apparently, he did it to fit in. As was later stressed by his defenders, the youth was merely trying to impress his peers and had found a decidedly bad means of doing it. With a few notables from the community vouching for his otherwise good character, the school eventually agreed to allow for James Buchanan's reinstatement. Buchanan came back a changed man and would end up graduating with honors. This was just one turning point in a life that would have many.

Chapter One

Life, Love, and Loss

"You have lost a child, a dear, dear child. I have lost the only earthly object of my affection. . . . I have now one request to make . . . Afford me the melancholy pleasure of seeing her body before internment."

—James Buchanan

After finishing up his education at Dickinson College, Buchanan decided to become an attorney. In furtherance of this cause, he moved to Lancaster, where he sought the tutelage of a seasoned lawyer by the name of James Hopkins. It is said that Buchanan took his understudy very seriously and spent long hours perfecting his craft.

Unlike today, aspiring attorneys did not necessarily have to hunker down in a law school. Back in Buchanan's time, more often than not, young men who wished to become an attorney simply formed a kind of apprenticeship with those that were already in practice. These long hours under his mentor evidently paid off because by the time Buchanan took his law examinations in 1812, he passed with flying colors.

Once his exams were behind him, he set out to start his own practice, setting up shop in a small office in Lancaster on February 20, 1813. His work took him all over Pennsylvania, where he would attend to legal matters involving contractual agreements, property, and handling the estates of the deceased. As his acclaim as an attorney grew, he was also made prosecutor of Lebanon County, a role which Buchanan's father hoped would have him showing "compassion and humanity for the poor creatures" that he might find himself prosecuting.

In the meantime, the War of 1812—the second major conflict between America and Britain after the American War of Independence—was in full force. The war inspired Buchanan to take the political situation of the nation more seriously. He became involved with the Federalist Party and began to advocate for the cause of having a centralized banking system, something which was anathema to many of the political leaders of the time, including the then-President James Madison.

As tensions grew, Buchanan became a vocal critic of the Madison administration. In particular, he lambasted the president over what he saw as failings of leadership during the war. As his political ambitions grew, Buchanan considered running for office himself, for a seat in the state legislature in 1814, but when he received word that the Brits had actually marched on Washington, D.C. and burned down the White House and Capitol building, he had second thoughts.

Instead of running for office, Buchanan ended up joining the military, taking part in the general mobilization in Lancaster, Pennsylvania, on August 25, 1814. Buchanan's unit became known as the Lancaster County Dragoons, and they were sent to shore up the defense of Baltimore, Maryland, which had recently seen quite a bit of action. Buchanan himself would see very little action, however, and by the time he arrived on the scene, the conflict was all but over.

Despite the disastrous loss of the White House and Capitol building, the Americans rallied to the cause and managed to drive the British out by December of that same year. Buchanan meanwhile managed to get a seat in the Pennsylvania House of Representatives. This would be the first office of many that James Buchanan would hold during his lifetime, and after a successful first term, he was easily re-elected.

Buchanan was rapidly rising to prominence in the social circles of Lancaster—so much so that in the fall of 1816, he was selected to be a manager at the annual society ball. This was a big deal for any up-and-coming socialite at the time. He also made sure to join his local chapter of the Freemasons since membership in such a fraternity was seen as a vital part for one that wanted to get together with the political elite. Buchanan joined up with the Masons in December of 1816.

As a member of more respectable society, Buchanan began to hang out at local pubs and taverns less and spend more time at the dinner parties of the upper crust. During these engagements, he would often hobnob with families who were seeking to find a match for their unmarried daughters. Buchanan proved quite good at these matchmaking affairs and was usually well-received. Soon enough, it was said that he was Lancaster's most eligible bachelor.

It was around this time that Buchanan made the acquaintance of a woman by the name of Ann Caroline Coleman. She was the daughter of an affluent industrialist by the name of Robert Coleman. James was first introduced to Ann in 1818 through an associate of his, Molton Rogers, who was dating Ann's cousin Eliza. Rogers had suggested that Buchanan "serve as an escort" for Ann during one of his outings with Eliza. In other words, Buchanan was invited to join his friend on a double date.

By all accounts, Buchanan was quite smitten by Ann, and by 1819, they were engaged to be married. Although Buchanan was initially received well enough, it is said that Ms. Coleman's parents had their doubts. It seems that Buchanan's reckless past had come back to haunt him, and tales of his riotous youth at Dickinson College was enough to make them reconsider him as a match for their daughter. This coupled with town gossip that Buchanan was more interested in Ann's family fortune than Ann herself began to sour the relationship.

It was during this tumultuous phase of the relationship that Buchanan made a misstep that Ann could not look past. He was away on business when he stayed with an associate of his by the name of William Jenkins and his wife. Mrs. Jenkins' niece, Grace Hubley, was also present at the time. Although it doesn't seem that anything untoward happened between Buchanan and Hubley, after the social circles of which Buchanan and Ms. Coleman were both a part received word of this visit, it was insinuated that Buchanan was attempting to court Miss Hubley.

This embarrassment was apparently the straw that broke the camel's back as far as Ann was concerned, and she abruptly broke off the engagement a short time later. Ann wouldn't live long after the engagement ended. The reason for her death is even more obscure than her reason for breaking it off with Buchanan. According to Buchanan's biographer Jean H. Baker, after the breakup, "this previously healthy twenty-three-year-old died suddenly of what one doctor diagnosed as 'hysterical convulsions.'"

Ann had apparently gone on a trip to visit her sister Margaret in order to get her mind off the turmoil in her life when she was struck with a terrible and sudden illness, which her doctor diagnosed as "female hysteria." She was prescribed Laudanum, an opium-based drug that was used for a whole range of conditions in those days. Shortly after, on December 9, 1819, Ann passed away.

Even though she had broken up with James Buchanan, when he heard the news of her passing, it is said that he was absolutely devastated. Buchanan managed to contact the girl's father and asked if he could attend the funeral, but he was steadfastly denied. The whole community of Lancaster was all aflutter with murmurings as to what may have happened. Some whispered that the girl had taken her own life; others suggested that she had lost her mind and died in an epileptic fit. Some even directly blamed Buchanan for her death. For his part, James Buchanan continued to maintain that his heart was broken, stating at the time, "I feel happiness has fled from me forever."

After the passing of Ann Coleman, Buchanan would never have a serious relationship with a woman again. In fact, he would eventually go down in history as the only American president to hold the office as a single bachelor. When questioned on this point, Buchanan always maintained that his love interest died with Ann Coleman. Later historians, however, would suggest that perhaps Buchanan had simply used the whole thing as a cover story, and he was never really much interested in romantic relationships with women in the first place. This, of course, is all just speculation, and no one really knows for sure.

At any rate, it was shortly after the death of Ann Coleman that Buchanan threw himself once again into the political arena. In 1820, he managed to secure a seat in the U.S. House of Representatives and, with it, a much-needed change of scenery. Buchanan would leave the rumor mills of Pennsylvania that had held him bound for a bold new life in Washington, D.C.

Chapter Two

A Man of Manifest Destiny

"Liberty must be allowed to work out its natural results; and these will, ere long, astonish the world."

—James Buchanan

On June 11, 1821, before the start of his first term in the House of Representatives, Buchanan received some terrible news. His father had been thrown from his horse-drawn carriage and perished from a mortal injury he sustained in the fall. James was devastated to hear of his father's passing, and he was even more distressed to find that his father had not left a will prior to his sudden death. This forced James Buchanan, as the eldest son, to take immediate action to make sure that his father's finances would be properly distributed among the rest of the family.

With this matter resolved, in November of that year, Buchanan left for Washington, D.C. He was a little dismayed upon his arrival to see that the new Capitol—which had been under construction since the old one had been burned down by the British—still left much to be desired. Nevertheless, he got to work, and during his first term, one of the most notable stances that Buchanan took was to take a stand against bankruptcy.

Congress had been debating the so-called Bankruptcy Bill championed by the Federalist John Sergeant. Buchanan was initially sought out by Sergeant for support, but Buchanan ended up joining the opposition. Making a long-winded speech, he highlighted what he perceived as the dangers of "bankruptcy privilege," which he believed would "destroy property because of the impossibility of controlling abuse of the privilege if it were extended to all classes." He also advised that any intrusion of the federal government in bankruptcy could only "lead to federal consolidation." Historians have since marked this moment as the beginning of Buchanan's steadfast belief in states' rights over federal intervention.

Many of the points that Buchanan argued would become important topics of debate in the upcoming 1824 presidential election. Initially, Buchanan supported former Secretary of War John C. Calhoun. Very quickly though, he was persuaded to back the much more dynamic character of Andrew Jackson.

Jackson was considered a war hero for his efforts as a general in the War of 1812. He was made the territorial governor of Florida in 1821, a U.S. senator in 1823, and by 1824, he was already running for president. Buchanan meanwhile was heading into his third term in Congress, and he was ready to do everything he could to help Jackson's campaign. Jackson, of course, would ultimately lose this contest to John Quincy Adams. Jackson would have to wait until 1828 to ultimately trounce Adams and gain the prize of the presidency for himself.

It was only after Jackson was elected in 1828 that he took note of Buchanan. Much like Jackson, Buchanan seemed to be a rising star of the Party, and by Jackson's second term in office, in 1832, he made Buchanan the U.S. ambassador to Russia. Buchanan was now a diplomat and, as such, he had to learn the language of the diplomats, which at that time was French.

At first glance, it might seem rather strange that Buchanan would have to learn French to speak to the Russians, but back then, French was widely spoken among the elite and was used as a kind of lingua franca in diplomatic circles. Once his mastery of French was deemed sufficient, Buchanan made his way to Russia, leaving in the spring of 1832 on a ship called the *Silas Richards*. Buchanan would not recall this particular excursion too fondly, remarking that he "suffered from seasickness during nearly the whole voyage."

Russia, being as far away as it was, would not be his first port of call, and on the way there, Buchanan's craft would make a pitstop in Britain. Here, Buchanan rested up and enjoyed the British nightlife for a few weeks before continuing on to Hamburg. It was from Hamburg that Buchanan finally set sail for St. Petersburg, arriving at the Russian capital on June 2. After being wined and dined by Russians for several days, Buchanan was introduced to the Russian tsar, Nicholas I. Buchanan would later recall how pleasantly surprised he was by the warmth and friendliness portrayed by the Russian ruler. It is said that he came right up to Buchanan, shook his hand, and expressed his desire for the diplomat to have a happy stay in the city.

During his time in Russia, Buchanan would mostly deal with issues in regard to commerce and trade. His shining moment came when he managed to help broker a lucrative trade agreement that permitted the U.S. to utilize the Russian-controlled Black Sea as a trade route. This was a real breakthrough for U.S. commerce in the region.

Buchanan's stay in Russia would last for about a year and a half. It's said that he didn't care too much for the climate, especially the fact that it was "chilly in June." The cold weather often left him feeling unwell despite his best efforts to adapt. Much more than the meteorological climate, however, Buchanan found himself considerably troubled by Russia's political climate.

At one point, he wrote a missive to then-President Jackson, informing him about the state on the ground, telling him, "there is no freedom of the press, no public opinion, and but little political conversation." Buchanan had very much enjoyed the relative liberty of the United States and was shocked to find the average Russian living in fear of their government. For a man who loved engaging in political debates, he found the Russian reticence to speak of politics disturbing.

By 1833, Buchanan was already thinking of heading back to America, and by August, he was given the opportunity to do so. Upon his homecoming to Pennsylvania, he found that for his family, life had moved on. Buchanan was somewhat dismayed to find that his sister Harriet had become married during his absence, without even bothering to tell him. Nevertheless, he tried to reassure his sister by telling her, "Do not for a moment suppose that I am offended; I am only disappointed. I confess I did not feel very anxious that you should be married. The indifference was no doubt partly selfish. I had often indulged the hope that we might spend the evening of our days together in my family."

Along with the changes made in his personal family, Buchanan found that the nation as a whole was likewise in flux. There had been a heated confrontation between the political factions of the day over banking and the so-called nullification crisis. The nullification crisis centered around the state of South Carolina, which, after balking at new tariffs created by the federal government, declared them "null and void" within South Carolina's state borders. The issue was a polarizing one, sending politicians scrambling to join one side or the other.

The fact that Buchanan had been out of the country and safely away from the fray proved to be politically expedient for him. He arrived just in time to begin campaigning for a U.S. Senate seat in his home state of Pennsylvania, none the worse for wear. The two most divisive issues of the time were over the nationalization of banks and slavery. It would be the latter that would come to haunt much of the rest of Buchanan's political career.

Buchanan, for his part, is said to have disliked slavery (although notably he did employ indentured servants), but at the same time, he believed that each individual state should choose whether or not it allowed the practice. He was such a steadfast supporter of states' rights that he was against any attempt by the federal government to outlaw slavery in the Southern states. Buchanan was also aware of just how serious Southerners were about keeping this tradition around. Buchanan fully believed that if the federal government stepped up to curtail slavery, the Southern states would go into an all-out rebellion. He was, of course, right in this assertion since this is essentially what happened at the end of his presidency in 1861.

Along with Buchanan's support of states' rights, he also proved to be a firm believer in the so-called "manifest destiny" of the United States. Manifest destiny was a popular concept in the mid-1800s, and the idea that the United States was destined to expand from its main base of settlement in the east all the way to the western coast was widely accepted. In furtherance of these goals, Buchanan made the case for America to annex both Texas and the western region that was then known as the Oregon Territory.

Buchanan would remain a strong voice in the U.S. Senate advocating for these measures to be taken, and by the presidential election of 1844, he briefly considered running for president himself. He backed away from the idea, however, when he realized that he just didn't have enough support at the time. Recognizing as much, he fell in line with the Democratic Party's chosen standard-bearer, James K. Polk. Just as he had done with Jackson, Buchanan actively supported the democratic candidate. Polk would ultimately win the contest, and just as Jackson had done several years before, Polk sought to reward Buchanan with a position in his administration.

In light of Buchanan's experience abroad in Russia, Polk decided to make Buchanan his secretary of state. It was through this role that Buchanan began to make his dreams of manifest destiny a reality. During Polk's presidency—which would only last one term—Buchanan was at the forefront of the efforts to expand the nation. The Oregon Territory, which had been occupied jointly by both the British and the Americans, was rather easily solved, with both sides amicably agreeing to divide the territory between themselves at the 49th parallel, thereby creating the modern border that still exists between the Pacific Northwest of the United States and Canada.

Among the new territorial acquisitions that Buchanan would oversee, it was Texas that would prove to be the most pressing. After Mexico gained independence from Spain in 1821, Texas was under the control of the Mexican government. The Mexican government proved to be unstable, however, and after demonstrating its inability to control northern territories such as Texas, the Texans seceded from Mexico and formed their own sovereign republic in 1836.

Soon thereafter, the Texans began to contemplate joining the United States, but the issue proved too divisive for American policymakers. The main problem centered around the fact that Texas allowed slavery. Since the United States was bitterly divided over the right of a state to have slaves, whenever a state entered the union, its status as a so-called "slave state" or "free state" would send one side or the other into an uproar.

Abolitionists from the North wanted no part of a large slaveholding state such as Texas, whereas the Southerners were clamoring to have Texas accepted into the Union since they saw Texas as a political ally. Ever since Texas gained independence from Mexico in 1836, the issue of bringing Texas into the Union proved to be so divisive that no president dared to touch it. That would all change under the stewardship of President Polk and his eager new secretary of state, James Buchanan.

Chapter Three

Buchanan in Britain

"What is right and what is practicable are two different things."

—James Buchanan

By 1845, most citizens of the Republic of Texas were becoming quite vocal about their desire to become part of the United States. Facing pressure from the Southern states as well as the Texans themselves, nearly ten years after Texas broke away from Mexico, President Polk was the U.S. president who finally allowed Texas to enter the Union.

It wasn't long after the admission of Texas that trouble began to brew on Texas' southern border with Mexico. Texans insisted that the border was much further south than the Mexicans believed it to be, and this led to border skirmishes. It was these skirmishes that culminated into the Mexican-American War. After some Americans were killed during the course of these border skirmishes, President Polk famously charged that the Mexicans had "shed American blood upon the American soil."

Riding high on this perceived grievance, Congress declared war shortly thereafter. Realizing that many around the world would think that the United States was trying to wage a war of conquest against Mexico, Buchanan drafted an official notice outlining that the U.S. was not seeking to "dismember Mexico but only to defend" the sovereignty of Texas. Polk did not agree with such limitations, however, and changed the memo to read, "We go to war with Mexico solely for the purpose of conquering an honorable peace." Such a revision would be important later on when Mexico was forced to cede valuable territory to its northwest.

The war began in the spring of 1846 and would last until 1848. The Mexican military proved to be in too much disarray to stand up to American forces, and after U.S. troops seized Mexico City, the Mexican government was forced to capitulate to American demands. This not only led to a new recognition of where Americans claimed the southern border of Texas was but also had Mexico coughing up major territorial concessions.

The locales that would eventually become California, Nevada, Arizona, and Utah, as well as big chunks of Colorado, Wyoming, and New Mexico, would all come about because of the terms of the so-called Treaty of Guadalupe Hidalgo. Signed in the Villa de Guadalupe Hidalgo, this one document granted the United States some 1.2 million square miles of land that had previously belonged to Mexico.

As successful as all this might seem, President Polk meanwhile made it known that he would not seek another term as president. And so, as the 1848 Presidential election loomed, the Democratic Party found itself scrambling to find another candidate to nominate for the election. Buchanan himself toyed with the idea of running but again realized that he didn't have enough support to make a realistic bid for the presidency.

In the end, it was a senator from Michigan by the name of Lewis Cass who would receive the nomination. Cass proved ill-equipped to run against the opposition—a war hero by the name of Zachary Taylor who led the charge in the Mexican-American War. Taylor easily won the presidential election. After this defeat for the Democratic Party, Buchanan's peers brokered the idea that Buchanan should try to get his old seat in the Senate back, but Buchanan had had enough of politics for a time.

Instead of going back into the political arena, he decided to buy some land just outside of Lancaster, Pennsylvania, and live a much quieter life. The property he acquired included a sprawling mansion called Wheatland, named after the surrounding wheat fields that were present when the estate was founded. Buchanan was in his late fifties at the time, and many were starting to wonder if the old bachelor would ever settle down and get married. If he was going to, this just might have been the perfect time for it.

Yet instead of finding a wife, Buchanan seemed more content in playing the part of family man with his extended family. He became close to many of his nieces and nephews during this period and helped them in whatever ways he could. It was his niece Harriet Lane whom he was the closest to, as Harriet's parents had died several years before, and Buchanan had essentially adopted her to raise as his own. He had paid her way in life, in the form of prestigious boarding schools, and now that he had a little time to spare, they began to spend much more of it together. Harriet, who was born in 1830, would have been around 18 at the time and just coming of age. Buchanan was determined to help her become a "proper lady" and provided her with all of the resources and connections she needed to succeed in life.

Buchanan contented himself to this quiet life at his country estate until events in 1852 would bring him back into the political arena. It was once again a presidential election year, and Buchanan's spirit became roused at the thought of once again ascending to the heights of the presidency. He set about positioning himself to become the Democratic nominee. He once again failed to garner enough support, however, and the nomination ultimately fell to fellow Democrat Franklin Pierce. Pierce would end up winning the election, and with his victory came another official appointment for Buchanan, as he was given the role of U.S. ambassador to the United Kingdom.

After setting his affairs in order at home, Buchanan made the fateful trip across the Atlantic to Britain in 1853. His favorite niece, Harriet Lane, would join him there the following year. It's interesting to note that even though it would be a few more years before Buchanan would become president and his niece would famously take on some of the traditional duties of the First

Lady, she was already taking on the role of a surrogate wife at the social functions that James Buchanan attended. Many Britons took note of Harriet's lively personality and were said to have been quite charmed by her. Queen Victoria herself is said to have been particularly taken by Buchanan's niece, enjoying her warm and friendly disposition.

Yet as well-received as Buchanan and his niece were at social functions in Britain, Buchanan found himself disappointed with his progress on the diplomatic front. One of his primary objectives at the time was to convince the British to give up any future designs in the Americas. As much as the British enjoyed the company of Buchanan, he found himself largely ignored and rebuffed on this issue.

One of the main points of contention was British efforts to create a canal through Central America that would make an easy water route from the Atlantic to the Pacific Ocean. This was still several decades before the Panama Canal would be created, and both the Americans and the British were in deep speculation over how such a feat could be done, and more importantly, who would have control of such a thing once it was created.

In 1850, the United States had entered into the Clayton-Bulwer Treaty, which outlined a situation that would give joint control over any canal that would be built. By the time Buchanan was in Britain, however, he continuously attempted to persuade the British to give up their designs in Central America and leave any future canal building solely in the hands of Americans.

Besides the issue of canal building in Central America, Buchanan was also tasked by the Pierce administration to speak with representatives of Spain about the possible acquisition of Cuba. The United States had long considered buying the island from the Spanish government, but Spain had so far not shown any interest in selling it. The Pierce administration thought they would take up the matter once again, and they sought to use Buchanan, their point man in Europe, to do it.

Buchanan met with Spanish ministers in Ostend, Belgium, to see if he could get the Spanish government interested in selling the territory, but once again, they demurred. Even though they failed to purchase Cuba, the Pierce administration would soon face political backlash when the discussions were made public. This was because many in the Northern states feared that Cuba, which already had slaves, would become another slave state, thereby strengthening the slaveholding South.

The slavery issue was still the most contentious aspect of American life, and by the time Buchanan returned to America in 1856, the country seemed poised to tear itself apart. The symptoms of terrible discord were spreading during the summer of 1856 and two incidents, in particular, were indicative of the volatility at play.

First, on May 22, after a heated debate in Congress, Southern Congressman Preston S. Brooks nearly beat to death a Northern senator by the name of Charles Sumner, right there on the Senate floor. Just two days after this assault, a radical abolitionist by the name of John Brown, who had been active in the struggle over "Bleeding Kansas" (discussed in a later chapter), led a deadly raid against pro-slavery Southerners in the region. It was on the night of May 24 that Brown and his men went door to door killing people in Pottawatomie Creek, Kansas.

James Buchanan was home once again, but the turmoil of his homeland left much to be desired.

Chapter Four

President Buchanan: The Early Years

"There is nothing stable but Heaven and the Constitution."

—James Buchanan

As the 1856 presidential election loomed near, Buchanan once again began to feel the waters for a possible run for the presidency. His old boss Pierce had fallen out of favor with the Democratic Party, and as such, they turned to James Buchanan as an able replacement. In the turmoil of the debate over slavery, Buchanan sought to position himself as a centrist and peacemaker between the two factions.

Buchanan, after all, sympathized with both sides. While he disliked slavery, he also believed that states should be able to choose their own destiny, and therefore believed that the federal government should not interfere in the affairs of the South. With this mentality in place, Buchanan sought to run for president in the 1856 election.

His opponent, Republican John C. Frémont, meanwhile, took a far more progressive approach that appealed to the North. He championed the construction of a Pacific railroad to help facilitate access to the new territories, particularly the new state of California, which the Republicans were hoping to secure support from. More importantly, he pledged to keep slavery from taking root in these new territories in the West.

Although many Northerners—most especially abolitionists—approved of Frémont's approach, the Southerners and conservatives in the North most certainly did not. Not willing to rock the boat, Buchanan took a much more cautious, middle-of-the-road approach during the election, and it worked. Buchanan ended up winning 174 electoral votes, while John C. Frémont only took 114.

Buchanan was pleased to have become president, but he arrived at the post with a very humble disposition. Upon being elected, he announced that he would not seek a second term in office. Even so, Buchanan knew that as the issue over slavery and states' rights heated up, he would be in for a rocky four years. Perhaps out of a desire to placate an increasingly restless South, Buchanan filled most of his cabinet positions with either Southerners or Southern sympathizers. This cabinet would prove highly influential with Buchanan, and since he was an unmarried bachelor, the men he worked with quickly became his main social circle.

Many historians contend that it was this very fact that caused Buchanan to become so oblivious to the tensions the slavery question was causing throughout the Union. Buchanan lived inside his own hand-picked bubble, blithely unaware that the polarization of the two sides was nearing a point of no return. As many still debated the best means of solving the crisis, Buchanan made clear his intention at his inauguration. He stood before those assembled and declared that the only solution to the conflict was "to leave the people of a territory free to decide their own destiny for themselves, subject only to the Constitution of the United States."

Shortly thereafter, the U.S. Supreme Court would reach a verdict in its landmark case of *Dred Scott v. Sandford*. The case was in regard to Dred Scott, a man who was born a slave but had been brought by his owners to the free states of Wisconsin and Illinois. Scott filed a lawsuit with the courts to gain his freedom since he had been brought to free states, where he, in his view, should automatically no longer be a slave. The case bounced around for several years until it finally reached the highest court in the land, the Supreme Court.

Unfortunately for Dred Scott, by the time his case reached the Supreme Court, it was packed with judges from the South, as well as Southern sympathizers. And in a move that would go down in infamy, the court ruled against Scott, stating that black people "are not included, and were not intended to be included, under the word 'citizens' in the Constitution, and can therefore claim none of the rights and privileges which that instrument provides for and secures to citizens of the United States." Although this move placated Southerners, it angered many in the North.

Nevertheless, Buchanan approved of the decision, touting it as being in line with his belief that neither the federal government nor the Supreme Court should interfere with determinations made at the state level. It would be his belief in "popular sovereignty"—that the people of the states should decide their own destiny—which would create so much bloodshed in the newly cobbled together territory of Kansas.

Kansas came about from the Kansas-Nebraska Act of 1854. There wasn't much question as to whether or not Nebraska would be a free state since it was so far north, but Kansas being geographically in the South raised some serious questions. As new settlers arrived, they brought their ideologies with them. Soon anti-slavery and pro-slavery forces were literally battling each other in a series of skirmishes that gave the region the nickname of "Bleeding Kansas."

In 1857, meetings were held in an attempt to create a state constitution, but the anti-slavery faction, feeling outnumbered by the pro-slavery forces, decided not to attend. With their boycott of the session, the pro-slavery faction had a free hand and saw to it that slavery was enshrined in the state constitution.

Once the constitution had been created, President Buchanan instructed Congress to allow Kansas to enter the United States as a slave state. However, since not all citizens of Kansas participated in the process, Congress did not honor it. It wouldn't be until the following year that Kansas would vote on the matter again. This time the anti-slavery faction had enough people present to vote against the institution of slavery and reject the previous constitution.

While this drama was playing out, the U.S. economy took a significant downturn. By 1857, many American businesses had gone belly up. As a result, many Americans lost their jobs and became unemployed. Many began to look toward the president for solutions to this problem, but Buchanan—ever the non-interventionist—did not feel that it was the place of the federal government to create job programs for the average American.

Making matters even worse, it was in that same year of 1857 that Buchanan had an unexpected insurrection flare up in Utah. The territory had been added in 1850 and, though not yet an official state, had many heading west to settle it. The most prominent group to come to the Utah territory by far were members of the Mormon faith. It was under the leadership of Brigham Young that the Mormon settlers began to militantly control access to the region and even allegedly harassed federal officers. It was this volatile situation that finally forced Buchanan's hand, and he sent in the troops in the summer of 1857.

The Utah rebellion would stand as the one insurrection that Buchanan successfully put down. Before his presidency was over, however, a whole host of Southern states would secede from the Union, and Buchanan would prove powerless to stop them.

Chapter Five

Diplomacy Abroad, Turmoil at Home

"The course of events is so rapidly hastening forward that the emergency may soon arise when you may be called upon to decide the momentous question whether you possess the power by force of arms to compel a state to remain in the Union."

—James Buchanan

The year 1858 was a pivotal one for the presidency of James Buchanan. The mid-terms were fast approaching, and the average citizen seemed just about as divided as the politicians who represented them. It was during this time that a rising star of the then quite young Republican Party—Abraham Lincoln—began to garner much attention for his spirited speeches and debates, especially his debates with a certain Democratic senator from Illinois by the name of Stephan A. Douglas.

Both Douglas and Lincoln would become standard-bearers for their respective parties in the 1860 presidential election and would become focal points of the tension playing out across the nation. But far outshining these political fireworks was the dangerous drama that would erupt at a place called Harpers Ferry in Virginia.

On October 17, 1859, the radical abolitionist John Brown along with 22 other men seized control of the Harpers Ferry armory with the intention of arming further partisans and sparking a full-scale rebellion against the slaveholding South. Buchanan was informed of these happenings shortly thereafter and quickly moved to mobilize a federal response that had the then-Colonel Robert E. Lee leading a group of marines in an assault on where John Brown and his followers were holed up.

Lee and his troops made short work of Brown and his would-be revolutionaries, and Brown himself was taken into custody. John Brown's raid, though largely a tactical failure, would prove quite useful in further fanning the flames of animosity between the North and South in the lead up to the American Civil War. John Brown and his raid served as yet another piece of the polarizing puzzle that America had become.

Southerners were outraged that Brown would attempt to spark a violent insurrection against their interests right in their own backyard. Northerners, on the other hand, while not always agreeing with Brown's use of force, were highly sympathetic to his cause. Many in the North felt that Brown was a good man, fighting the good fight against slavery; they just may not have agreed that laying siege to federal property was the best way of going about doing it.

Nevertheless, for those that called Brown a villain and those who raised him up as a hero, after his failed raid, the divide between North and South had become more readily apparent than ever before. After a short trial, John Brown was executed for his role in the Harpers Ferry raid, becoming nothing short of a martyr and his name a rallying cry for those that advocated shaking off the yoke of slavery.

As the nation became more and more polarized, the centrist position of James Buchanan became all the less tenable. In the end, it would be Illinois Senator Stephen A. Douglas who would secure the presidential nomination. Southerners—not approving of his nomination—

turned to Buchanan's own vice president, John C. Breckinridge, instead. Diluting the vote even further, prominent Tennessee politician John Bell threw his hat into the ring as well.

In the lead-up to the final vote, Buchanan was distracted by his diplomatic duties as president. It was around this time that a special envoy from Japan had arrived in the U.S. to sign a historic treaty with the United States. This was the first Japanese delegation to set foot on American soil, and Buchanan was the president who oversaw it all.

Also in attendance was Buchanan's niece, Harriet Lane. Harriet was quite fascinated by the Japanese visitors and remarked at the time, "They are really a curiosity. All the women seem to run daft about them." Buchanan himself was later remembered rather fondly by the delegation with the Vice Ambassador Muragaki Norimasa, who recalled President Buchanan as having "a genial manner without losing noble dignity."

Despite the polarization in the United States at the time, Congress managed to appropriate some $50,000 for the affair, complete with lavish dinners and gold medals for the delegates. The meeting was largely a success, and the treaty signed would remain in force for nearly 40 years.

In the midst of all of the domestic turmoil that erupted in the U.S. in 1860, it's easy to overlook this unique Japanese mission that had arrived on American shores, but it stands as one of the most successful moments of Buchanan's presidency.

This diplomatic feat was followed up by another first when Buchanan arranged for the prince of Wales (future King Edward VII) to visit him at the White House. The British delegation was on their way to Canada, which was still under British control, and it was only by way of Buchanan's own personal suggestion to Queen Victoria that it was arranged for the prince to head down to the United States at the conclusion of his Canadian visit. This momentous occasion would be very meaningful for several reasons.

First of all, it was historic since it was the first time that a British royal paid a visit, and secondly, it would signify the general relaxation of tension between the two nations. The United States had been in a knockdown drag-out fight with Britain less than 100 years before during the War of Independence. A few decades later, the War of 1812 had Britain and the United States again at each other's throats.

Both the Japanese delegation and the visit of the British prince serve as a testimony to the diplomatic capability of James Buchanan. But whatever skills he had may have had with diplomacy abroad, they would be forever marred when his diplomatic wrangling at home altogether failed in what would become a bloody and bitter civil war.

Chapter Six

The Outbreak of the Civil War

"All the friends that I loved and wanted to reward are dead, and all the enemies that I hated and I had marked out for punishment are turned to my friends."

—James Buchanan

As election day neared, it became a four-way race between two Democrats—Buchanan's Vice-President Breckinridge and Illinois Senator Stephen A. Douglas—along with John Bell from the Constitutional Union Party and the Republican candidate, Abraham Lincoln. This match-up would result in Lincoln winning nearly all of the Northern states, including Buchanan's home state of Pennsylvania, whereas Breckinridge picked off most of the Southern states. Bell gained three states, and Douglas won only two.

In this four-way race, Lincoln would come out in the lead with 180 electoral votes. This was apparently quite contrary to what Buchanan hoped the outcome to be. Buchanan believed that the split would work in the Democrats' favor, with Douglas peeling off votes from the North while Breckinridge gained just enough support in the South for a majority. Obviously, this is not what happened.

Shortly before the results came in, Buchanan had stressed his strong reservations over a Lincoln presidency, declaring, "Should Lincoln be elected, I fear troubles enough though I have been doing all I can by conversations to prevent them." This statement is indicative of the fact that Buchanan saw himself as keeping the peace by appeasing the South. He feared that someone such as Lincoln, who was seen as being sympathetic to the abolition of slavery, would undo all of the steps of concession that Buchanan believed he had made.

Viewed through a modern lens, and indeed even just shortly after the American Civil War itself, most would interpret things quite differently. Rather than seeing Buchanan's efforts to placate the South as being for the greater good, most historians would come to view his appeasement as contributing to the war, rather than heading it off at the pass.

At any rate, upon the election of Abraham Lincoln in November of 1860, outgoing President James Buchanan found his worst fears come to fruition. Just days after Lincoln secured his electoral victory, several Southern states were openly speaking of secession. At the same time, Buchanan's own cabinet, which included prominent Southerners, were beginning to show where their true loyalties were, rejecting Buchanan's pleas for restraint in favor of solidarity with their home states back in the South.

It wasn't until the third week of November that Buchanan ended his long silence on the growing calamity. As Southern states murmured about their intention to leave the Union, Buchanan announced that he would "deny any right of secession and oppose it strongly." Buchanan still sympathized with the South for what he perceived as ill-treatment at the hands of the North, but even so, he made it clear that he felt that none of these perceived wrongs justified leaving the Union.

He furthermore stressed that Lincoln was legally elected, and as president-elect, Lincoln had not even yet had the chance to do anything to provoke their ire. He reasoned that unless Lincoln were to commit "some overt and dangerous act," there was no reason for such an overreaction on their part. He also furthermore stressed to the Southerners that Lincoln and the Republicans were the minority in both houses of Congress and could not unilaterally change their way of life without the support of Congress.

Nevertheless, the fear of Lincoln among Southerners was so great that they wouldn't even wait for the man to be sworn into office before they began to leave the Union. The first state to secede was South Carolina, which officially left the Union on December 20, 1860.

On the very day of South Carolina's secession, James Buchanan is said to have been at a wedding reception. Buchanan suddenly noticed a commotion break out among some of the guests and asked a woman next to him, "Madam, do you suppose the house is on fire?" But it wasn't the house that was on fire—it was the Union. After the woman went to see what the commotion was about, she returned to promptly report that the other guests had just received via telegram the news that South Carolina had officially departed from the United States of America.

Upon hearing the news, Buchanan immediately called for his carriage and headed to the White House where he found the same exact news waiting for him, announcing that the newly elected governor of South Carolina—Francis Wilkinson Pickens—had indeed just sent his state hurtling out of the Union. The most troubling aspect of all this was the fact that a military base in South Carolina, Fort Sumter, was still manned by federal troops even while the surrounding state had just rebelled against the American government.

Fearing that Fort Sumter would be taken, on the day after Christmas—December 26, 1860—Major Robert Anderson who had been assigned to nearby Fort Moultrie took the initiative of bolstering Fort Sumter's defenses by relocating two whole companies of troops and armaments to Fort Sumter. This was all done of his own initiative without seeking approval from President Buchanan. Buchanan, who was still seeking to negotiate with South Carolina, was infuriated at the move since he feared it would only escalate matters even further.

Shortly thereafter, Buchanan was paid a visit by none other than the then-senator from Mississippi (soon to be Confederate president),

Jefferson Davis. In light of the military maneuvering at Fort Sumter, Davis struck an accusatory tone as he chastised Buchanan, "Now, Mr. President, you are surrounded with blood and dishonor on all sides." Buchanan was both apologetic and downright apoplectic as he railed, "My God, are calamities never to come singly! I call God to witness, you gentlemen more than anybody know that this is not only without but against my orders. It is against my policy."

Nevertheless, despite his initial attempt to wash his hands of the matter, on January 9, 1861, Buchanan tried to relieve the beleaguered defenders of Fort Sumter. On that day, a merchant steamer called the *Star of the West* was loaded up with food and supplies in New York and sent to sail down to South Carolina. This type of ship was specifically chosen so that it could avoid notice and even potentially be passed off as a regular commercial craft. Nevertheless, the Southern militias were ready for the *Star of the West*, and after a barrage erupted from defensive batteries that they had put in place, the ship was forced to retreat.

The fact that Buchanan was seemingly powerless in the face of this aggression would only embolden further secession. It was on the very day that the *Star of the West* was beaten back to the North that the state of Mississippi decided to secede. South Carolina and Mississippi were then joined by Florida on January 10, Alabama on January 11, Georgia on January 19, Louisiana on January 26, and Texas on February 1. On February 9, Jefferson Davis, the former senator from Mississippi who had upbraided Buchanan over Fort Sumter, was made the president of what became known as the Confederate States of America.

By March, James Buchanan was preparing to hand over the keys of command to president-elect Lincoln, even while the Union was falling apart all around him. At this point, Buchanan may very well have felt like the captain of a sinking ship, but he was just as determined not to go down with it.

Chapter Seven

Life after the Presidency

"I feel that my duty has been faithfully, though it may be imperfectly, performed, and, whatever the result may be, I shall carry to my grave the consciousness that I at least meant well for my country."

—James Buchanan

Abraham Lincoln was sworn into office on March 4, 1861. The days before his inauguration were full of tumult and conspiratorial intrigue between various political factions in the nation. There was even a rumor floating around that there were those who sought to assassinate Lincoln before he became president. Buchanan, aware of this turmoil, requested extra troop placements to have extra protection on hand for Lincoln's inauguration day.

It is said that on the very day that Buchanan was preparing to pass the torch to Lincoln, he received a troubling message from Major Anderson at Fort Sumter. Anderson, who had taken the unilateral action of reinforcing Sumter without Buchanan's orders, was now demanding that another 20,000 troops be sent to better defend the installation from potential Southern incursions. Buchanan, however, was ready to wash his hands of the matter and, putting the message from Anderson to the side, he prepared himself to meet Abraham Lincoln on the White House grounds.

A reporter that covered this momentous occasion remarked of Buchanan's disposition, that he "appeared pale and wearied; yet his face beamed with radiance, for he felt relieved from the crushing care and anxiety he had borne for four years." Buchanan himself perhaps summed up his sentiment best when, after greeting Lincoln, he remarked, "My dear sir, if you are as happy in entering the White House as I shall feel on returning to Wheatland, you are a happy man indeed."

Buchanan was indeed looking forward to moving out of Washington, D.C. and going back to his country estate in Pennsylvania. He was ready to allow someone else to shoulder responsibility and blame for the events that ensued. Yet even though Buchanan left office, the recriminations against him would not altogether cease.

After the inauguration, Buchanan and his entourage got on a train and headed for Lancaster, Pennsylvania. Upon his arrival, Buchanan was given a traditional 34-gun presidential salute followed by the ringing of church bells. As much as he would be later scorned, his initial homecoming was rather affectionate. His first month home in Wheatland was one of great relief, as Buchanan enjoyed a steady stream of visitors and well-wishers.

Lincoln meanwhile was fully aware of the ticking time bomb that he had inherited and had been briefed that the besieged Fort Sumter would run out of supplies by April 15. Realizing that he had to act, Lincoln sent several ships, including the USS *Pawnee*, USS *Powhatan*, USS *Pocahontas*, and even a craft named after Buchanan's niece—the USRC *Harriet Lane*—to bolster the ailing fort.

On April 12, meanwhile, Confederate troops fired on Fort Sumter in what would be the opening shots of the American Civil War. After the war began in earnest, Buchanan, who had previously sympathized with the South, made his allegiance clear by condemning the attack on Fort Sumter. He also urged his fellow Pennsylvanians to enlist in the army in support of the Union.

His support of the cause of the North was viewed as too little too late for most, and Buchanan—long remembered for his inaction when he was president—began to receive regular hate mail which railed against him as the cause of the current crisis. Even worse, once the war was in full force, a Senate resolution was compiled on December 15, 1862, which essentially placed all the blame on Buchanan's soldiers.

The resolution declared, "After it had become manifest that an insurrection against the United States was about to break out in several of the Southern States, James Buchanan, then President, form sympathy with the conspirators and their treasonable project, failed to take necessary and proper measures to prevent it; wherefore he should receive the censure and condemnation of the Senate and the American people."

As the blows continued to rain down upon Buchanan, it not only took a psychological toll on the ex-president but also a physical one as Buchanan began to suffer from fits of nervous exhaustion due to the stress and strain that he was under. As 1863 and 1864 proved to be the bloodiest years of the war, Buchanan found himself becoming more and more of an apologist for his actions. Critics meanwhile lashed out at him over every contrived grievance under the sun. At one point, the press in New York even charged Buchanan as having stolen portraits from the White House and accused him of pocketing all of the gifts brought by the Japanese delegation of 1860.

Buchanan tried to defend himself by explaining that the portraits were of the British royal family and given to him by Queen Victoria. He also denied making away with the gifts bestowed by the Japanese delegation, save for "a couple of stuffed birds" for his niece Harriet. Yet no matter how much he tried to defend himself, for his detractors, his explanations always fell short.

Feeling increasingly cornered and isolated, Buchanan began to write a book as an explanation of his actions before the carnage began. The text came with the rather self-explanatory title of *Mr. Buchanan's Administration on the Eve of Rebellion*. The book would be published in 1866, a year after the bloodshed of the Civil War had ended, and Abraham Lincoln had already been assassinated. Buchanan was hoping for vindication through the biography he crafted, but history still had much to be written.

Conclusion

After spending years struggling with his health, as well as his reputation, Buchanan caught a bad cold in the early summer of 1868, eventually passing away of respiratory failure on June 1 at 77 years of age. He died in his Wheatland estate with those that knew and loved him best by his side.

In his last days, Buchanan often declared that history would vindicate him. He would be rather saddened to find out that this simply wasn't the case. Nearly 160 years after he left office, James Buchanan is quite regularly ranked as one of the worst presidents in the history of the United States. He is generally viewed as an appeaser who emboldened the South through his inaction and passivity. Of all the presidents that were ever elected, James Buchanan came to office during one of the most tumultuous periods in American history. Unfortunately, he failed to step up to the plate, and the nation was plunged into a bloody civil war.

Bibliography

Baker, Jean H. (2004). *James Buchanan.*

Buchanan, James (1866). *Mr Buchanan's Administration on the Eve of the Rebellion.*

Curtis, George Ticknor (1883). *Life of James Buchanan: Fifteenth President of the United States.*

Greenstein, Fred I. (2013). *Presidents and the Dissolution of the Union: Leadership Style from Polk to Lincoln.*

Holzer, Harold (2008). *Lincoln: President-Elect.*

Klein, Philip S. (1962). *President James Buchanan: A Biography.*

Potter, David Morris (1976). *The Impending Crisis, 1848–1861.*

Strauss, Robert (2016). *Worst. President. Ever.: James Buchanan, the POTUS Rating Game, and the Legacy of the Least of the Lesser Presidents.*